Table of Contents

Serves 6 - 10

- ½ cup unsalted butter
- ¼ cup all-purpose flour
- 2 Tbsp. tomato puree
- 1 onion, finely chopped
- ½ cup green pepper, finely chopped
- 1 stalk celery, finely chopped
- 6 green onions, chopped
- 2 cloves garlic, minced
- 2 lbs. crawfish tail, whole
- 1 tsp. cayenne pepper
- 2 egg whites
- 2 Tbsp. water
- ¼ cup cream

PASTRY DOUGH

- 2 cups all-purpose flour
- ½ tsp. salt
- ¼ tsp. sugar
- ½ cup unsalted butter, cold
- 3 Tbsp. shortening, cold
- ¼ cup cold water

Pastry: Prepare 1 day ahead and refrigerate. Combine flour, salt and sugar in a bowl. Cut in the butter and shortening until mixture resembles coarse crumbs. Stir in the cold water until dough holds together. If needed, you may add 1 additional tablespoon of water. Cover and refrigerate over night.

Roux for filling: Melt butter in saucepan over medium heat. Whisk in ¼ cup of flour. Cook, stirring frequently, until roux turns dark golden brown (about 30 minutes). Add tomato puree, onion, bell pepper, celery, green onions and garlic. Reduce heat and cook, covered, for 1 hour, stirring occasionally. Stir in the crawfish and cayenne pepper. Uncover and cook additional 20 minutes to reduce liquid. Add salt to taste, remove from heat and let stand for 30 minutes.

Lightly flour cutting board or counter. Roll out ¼ of pastry into a circle ¼ inch thick. Using a 4½ inch round biscuit cutter press out circles. Reserve trimmings. Spoon 1 tablespoon of filling onto ½ of the pastry circle. Beat egg whites with water and brush edge of each circle. Fold in half and seal edge with fork. Dredge each pie in flour and place on greased baking sheet. Repeat until all dough and filling is used. Brush each pie with cream and bake in 400° F oven for 25 minutes or until golden brown.

Serves 4 - 6

- 4 slices bacon
- 1 onion, finely chopped
- ¼ cup celery, finely chopped
- 2 Tbsp. bell pepper, finely chopped
- 1½ cups fish stock
- 2 cups potatoes, peeled and diced
- 1 lb. crawfish tails
- 2 cups heavy cream
- 2 tsp. butter
- • cayenne and parsley to garnish

Brown bacon in 3 qt. saucepan. Remove from pan, crumble and reserve. Add onions, celery and bell pepper to bacon fat. Sauté vegetables until tender. Add fish stock, potatoes and bacon. Cook over medium heat until potatoes are tender. Add crawfish and simmer covered over low heat for 10 minutes. Just before serving, add cream, stirring until cream is heated through. Be careful not to allow cream to curdle. Sprinkle servings with cayenne and parsley. Serve immediately.

Boiled Crawfish

Serves 4

- 6 lbs. crawfish, live if available
- • cold salted water
- 1 cup salt
- 6 lemons, quartered
- 2 stalks celery, chopped
- 4 yellow onions, quartered
- 3 russet potatoes, quartered
- 5 bay leaves
- 1 tsp. dried thyme
- 4 bags crab boil
- 1 Tbsp. cayenne pepper
- 2 whole heads of garlic, broken in half
- 5 quarts water
- 2 cups cold water
- • fresh lemons, quartered

If live crawfish are available they will need to be rinsed well. Start by soaking them in cold water for 12 hours. Drain, rinse and repeat the soaking process until water is clear of any mud. In a 3-gallon stockpot combine 6 quarts cold water with vegetables and seasonings and bring to a boil. Boil for 15 minutes, then add the crawfish. Add more water if necessary; the water should just cover the crawfish. Return to boil and cook for 10 - 12 minutes. After cooking time has expired remove from heat and add 2 cups cold water and let stand at room temperature for 10 minutes. Drain crawfish in colander, reserving onions and potatoes.

Serving instructions: Cover table with sheets of waxed paper and top with plenty of newspaper. Place crawfish in center of table along with fresh lemon wedges and the vegetables piled on plates. Each person takes a crawfish from the pile. Twist and separate the tail from the rest of the crawfish. The head may be discarded. Some enthusiasts enjoy tasting the spices in the body and "suck the head". Peel off a couple of bands of shell at the tail opening. Gently pinch along length of the tail to loosen meat. At the end of the tail firmly pinch while pulling the meat from the tail. Pop into mouth or first dunk into sauce of your choice.

Cajun Rib Eye with Crawfish Sauce

Serves 4

- 1 cup vegetable oil
- 1 onion, thinly sliced
- 3 tsp. garlic powder
- 1 Tbsp. coarse ground pepper
- 4 10-oz. rib-eye steaks
- 1 Tbsp. paprika
- 1½ tsp. cayenne pepper
- 1 tsp. salt

Sauce:

- 2 scallions, minced
- 1 clove garlic, minced
- 2 Tbsp. butter
- ¼ tsp. cayenne
- ½ cup port wine
- ½ cup crawfish tails
- 1½ cups beef broth
- 1½ Tbsp. cornstarch
- 1 Tbsp. cold water

Combine oil, onion, garlic powder and 1 tablespoon coarse ground pepper in resealable plastic bag. Add steaks to marinade and coat both sides completely. Cover and refrigerate 8 hours or overnight. Remove steaks from marinade and discard bag. Combine remaining dry ingredients. Sprinkle each side of steaks evenly with combined spices. Grill steaks over hot coals, 8 minutes total for medium-rare.

Sauté scallions, garlic, butter and cayenne in small saucepan for 1 minute. Add wine, crawfish tails, and beef broth. Return to rolling boil for 3 minutes. Mix cornstarch and water together and add to sauce while stirring until thickened. Serve over grilled steaks and garnish with sliced scallion tops.

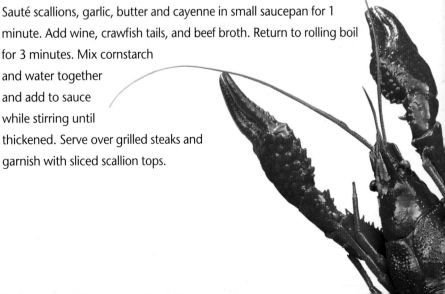

Creamy Crawfish Enchiladas

Serves 6

For the Sauce:

1   Tbsp. lard or bacon fat
1   tsp. chili powder
¼   cup onion, finely chopped
2   Tbsp. green bell pepper, finely chopped
2   Tbsp. celery, finely chopped
1   tsp. garlic, finely chopped
¼   cup fish stock or clam juice
¾   cup whipping cream
1½ tsp. corn flour
¼   cup cheddar cheese, shredded
•   salt to taste

For Assembly:

6   6" corn tortillas
12 oz. crawfish tails, cooked & chopped
1   Tbsp. green onion, chopped
⅓   cup monterey jack cheese, shredded

To prepare the sauce: Melt lard in a medium saucepan; add chili powder, onion, bell pepper, celery and garlic. Cook over medium heat until soft (about 10 minutes). Add corn flour and cook 2 minutes more. Add cream and stock, bringing mixture to a boil. Add cheddar cheese, stirring constantly until fully melted. Remove sauce from heat and season to taste with salt. Heat oven to 400° F, then prepare the enchiladas. Soften tortilla shells by wrapping them in plastic wrap and heating them in the microwave oven for 30 - 50 seconds. Combine half the sauce with the crawfish tails. Fill each tortilla shell with ¼ cup of this mixture and sprinkle with green onion. Roll shells around filling and fit snugly into a small baking dish. Pour remaining sauce over all and top with shredded monterey jack. Bake until enchiladas are heated through and cheese is melted and bubbly (about 10 - 15 minutes).

Cajun Style Vegetable Salad

Serves 6

1   medium onion, thinly sliced
2   Tbsp. unsalted butter
1   Tbsp. vegetable oil plus oil to fry okra
3   cups (4 ears) fresh corn kernels including scrapings
1   tomato, seeded & chopped
½   cup heavy cream
¼   cup water
¼   lb. okra rinsed and patted dry, sliced ¼" thick
1   cup cornmeal seasoned with pepper, for coating okra

In a heavy saucepan cook the onion in the butter and 1 tablespoon of oil over moderate heat, stirring occasionally, until golden. Add the corn, tomato, cream and the water. Cook the mixture, covered over moderately low heat, stirring occasionally, for 20 minutes. Season corn mixture with salt and pepper and keep the mixture warm and covered. Toss okra in a bowl with seasoned cornmeal. Shake into a coarse sieve to remove excess cornmeal. In a deep skillet heat ½-inch of the additional oil over moderately high heat until oil is hot but not smoking. Fry the okra in batches for 1 to 2 minutes, or until it is golden. Transfer with a slotted spoon to paper towels to drain. Serve the corn mixture topped with the fried okra.

Crawfish Fried Rice

Serves 6

2   cups long-grain rice
1   onion, chopped
1   bell pepper, chopped
1   clove garlic, finely chopped
½   cup green onions, chopped
¼   cup parsley separate stems from leaves, finely chopped
2   cups crawfish tails, washed
¼   cup Louisiana style hot pepper sauce
•   salt to taste

Ahead of time, cook the long grain rice and chill. In wok or large skillet, sauté onions, bell pepper, garlic and parsley stems in oil until crisp-tender over high heat. Add washed crawfish, green onions and parsley leaves. Sauté for another 2 - 3 minutes. Mix cooked rice and crawfish together, adding pepper sauce. Keep stirring until rice is heated through. Salt to taste.

Crawfish Monseigneur

Serves 6

2   lbs. crawfish tails
½   tsp. cayenne
6   shakes hot pepper sauce
¼   cup butter, salted
2   cups fresh mushrooms, sliced
¼   cup pimentos
4   green onion tops, sliced
¾   cup white wine
1½   Tbsp. cornstarch
2   Tbsp. water
½   cup half and half
16   oz. angel hair pasta, cooked

Sprinkle crawfish tails with cayenne and pepper sauce. Melt butter in heavy skillet over medium heat. Sauté crawfish for 3 - 4 minutes. Add mushrooms, pimentos and scallion tops. Lower heat, cover and sauté for 5 minutes. Remove cover and add wine. Mix cornstarch, water and half and half together. Slowly add to crawfish mixture and continue stirring until mixture reaches a slow boil. Simmer uncovered for 8 - 10 minutes, stirring occasionally. Serve over hot pasta.

Boiled Rice

Serves 4

1   cup long-grain white rice
2   cups cold water
1   tsp. salt
1   tsp. salted butter

Combine all ingredients in heavy 3-quart saucepan. Cover with a tight-fitting lid and bring to a boil over high heat. Stir once, then cover tightly and reduce heat to very low. Set a timer for 15 minutes and allow rice to cook, covered. Then remove pan from heat, uncover and fluff with a fork.

Crawfish Monica

Serves 4

2	cups chopped onion
1	cup celery, chopped
1	cup parsley, chopped
2	lbs. peeled crawfish tails
24	oz. fettuccine, cooked
2	cups heavy cream
½	lb. butter
1	tsp. basil, finely chopped
½	tsp. dried thyme
½	tsp. dried oregano
½	tsp. cayenne pepper
½	tsp. freshly ground pepper

Melt butter in large skillet or sauté pan. Sauté onion and celery until soft (about 5 minutes). Add remaining ingredients, except pasta, and simmer for 15 minutes. Place large serving bowl in 200° F oven for 10 minutes. Add pasta to warmed bowl and toss with sauce.

Gumbo Ya Ya

Serves 8 - 10

1	chicken, cut up in small pieces
2	Tbsp. Creole seasoning
2	cups flour
¾	cup vegetable oil
2	medium onions, diced
1	cup celery, diced
2	cups bell pepper, diced
6	cups chicken broth
3	cloves garlic, minced
1	lb. crawfish tails
1	lb. andouille sausage

Dredge chicken in flour. Heat oil in large heavy skillet and brown chicken pieces. Remove chicken and reserve in warm oven. Add remaining flour to oil to make roux. Stir consistently, loosening any particles stuck to pan. Continue to stir and cook roux until a dark brown appearance is achieved. Add onions, celery and bell pepper and cook until vegetables are tender. Add stock to mixture and bring to a boil. Add garlic, crawfish tails and sausage. Reduce heat, cover and simmer until chicken is tender, (about 40 minutes). Serve over rice.

Bayou Grilled Chicken

Serves 6

½	cup fresh lemon juice
¼	cup hot pepper sauce
¼	cup olive oil
3	Tbsp. red wine vinegar
3	Tbsp. Cajun seasoning, no salt
6	bone-in chicken breasts
1	large onion, peeled and quartered
2	small zucchini squash

Combine spices and liquids in a resealable plastic bag to create marinade. Scrub zucchini and slice lengthwise in ¼-inch slices, leaving peel on. Add chicken and vegetables, seal bag, and gently coat all pieces. Place bag in refrigerator for 2 hours and allow flavors to seep through. Remove chicken from marinade and grill over medium coals, turning often to discourage skin from burning. Place vegetables in grilling basket or on skewers and place on grill with chicken for about the last 6 - 8 minutes. Grill chicken until fully cooked, internal temperature of thickest part of breast should reach 165° F. Vegetables should be crisp but tender.

11

Broiled Garlic Oysters

Serves 4

24	oysters, on the half shell
1	Tbsp. fresh parsley, chopped fine
•	sea salt, to taste
4	oz butter
•	fresh ground black pepper, to taste
3	cloves fresh garlic, crushed
6	scallions, finely chopped

Place oysters on rock salt covered broiler pan. Preheat broiler. Over low heat sauté parsley, salt, pepper, garlic and butter, until butter is fully melted. Spoon butter mixture over the oysters. Place oysters under broiler until heated and oysters begin to curl, (about 3 minutes). Serve warm.

Oyster Pâté

Serves 6

12	oz. cream cheese
½	small onion
2	scallions
1	can smoked oysters, drained
2	tsp. paprika
1	tsp. salt
¼	tsp. cayenne

Clean and coarsely chop onion and scallions and place in food processor. Process onions until finely chopped. Add cream cheese and paprika and process until mixture is well incorporated. Scrape edges of bowl; add oysters, cayenne and salt and process again, just until smooth. Form into ball or loaf and roll in finely chopped pecans or parsley. Refrigerate for 2 hours and serve with party crackers.

Oysters Rockefeller

12	oysters, whole
12	oz. beer
2	cloves garlic
2	Tbsp. Creole seasoning
•	seasoning salt to taste
7	black peppercorns
½	cup butter
1	onion, chopped
1	clove crushed garlic
1	(10 oz) package frozen chopped spinach, thawed and drained
4	oz. shredded monterey jack cheese
4	oz. fontina cheese, shredded
4	oz. mozzarella cheese
¼	cup milk
•	hot pepper sauce
2	tsp. salt
1	tsp. ground black pepper
2	Tbsp. fine bread crumbs, optional

Clean oysters and place in a large stockpot. Add the beer and enough water to cover oysters, creole seasoning, garlic, seasoning salt and peppercorns. Bring to boil. Remove from heat, drain and cool oysters. Preheat oven to 400° F. Separate shells on cooled oysters, leaving oysters on one half. Place oysters on a baking sheet covered with sea salt or rock salt to stabilize them. In large saucepan sauté onion and garlic in butter until softened. Stir in spinach and cheeses until cheese has melted. Add milk, salt and pepper, stirring until well blended. Add hot pepper sauce to taste. Spoon sauce over each oyster, just filling the shell. Sprinkle with bread crumbs and bake until golden and bubbly. Serve immediately.

Artichoke Oyster Soup

Serves 6 to 8

6	Tbsp. butter, melted
½	cup scallions
¼	tsp. thyme
1	bay leaf
½	tsp. cayenne pepper
2	Tbsp. flour
14	oz. chicken broth
4	cups oysters, drained (reserving liquid)
14	oz. artichoke hearts, drained
2	tsp. salt
¼	tsp. hot pepper sauce
½	cup whipping cream
3	Tbsp. fresh parsley, chopped

In medium saucepan or stockpot sauté scallions in butter until wilted. Add thyme, bay leaf, cayenne and flour. Whisk until flour is well incorporated. Add chicken broth, reserved oyster liquid, quartered artichoke hearts and hot pepper sauce. Bring to boil while stirring constantly. Place oysters and parsley into boiling broth, lower heat slightly and simmer for not more than 5 minutes. Add whipping cream, stir, and remove from heat. Serve immediately.

Oyster, Eggplant & Mushroom Casserole

Serves 6

2	medium eggplants
2	pints fresh-shucked oysters
¾	cup butter, divided
8	oz. fresh mushrooms, sliced
¼	cup scallions, sliced
½	tsp. hot pepper sauce
¼	cup parsley, chopped
4	cloves garlic, finely chopped
1	tsp. dried basil
½	tsp. ground thyme
•	salt to taste
1	cup Cheddar cheese, grated
½	cup evaporated milk
½	cup breadcrumbs

Pierce eggplants several times with a fork and place on a baking sheet. Preheat oven to 350° F and bake 30 to 50 minutes or until very tender. Remove from oven and cool. While eggplant is cooling, heat oysters and their liquid until edges begin to curl. Remove oysters with slotted spoon and set aside. Add to the oyster liquid ¼ cup butter, mushrooms and 2 tablespoons scallions. Simmer 10 minutes or until reduced to ½ cup liquid. Chop remaining oysters and add to saucepan. Add ½ cup breadcrumbs and hot pepper sauce; mix well. Melt ¼ cup butter in sauté pan and sauté remaining scallions for 5 minutes. Add parsley, garlic, remaining bread-crumbs, basil, thyme and salt. Mix well and set aside. Peel eggplants and slice into ¼ inch slices. Cover the bottom of an oblong, shallow baking dish with eggplant slices. Cover eggplant with half of breadcrumbs and herb mixture and half of oyster mixture. Repeat with remaining eggplant, breadcrumbs and oyster mixtures. Sprinkle cheese over the top and drizzle the evaporated milk over cheese. Sprinkle lightly with breadcrumbs and dot with remaining butter. Bake in a preheated 350° F oven for 20 minutes or until cheese has melted.

13

Spicy Oysters

Serves 4

3 plum tomatoes, seeded and diced
3 green onions, chopped
⅓ cup fresh cilantro, chopped
2 Tbsp. olive oil
2 tsp. ground cumin
2 jalapeño or Anaheim peppers, seeded & chopped
12 fresh oysters shucked, left on shell
• crusty French bread

Combine first 6 ingredients in medium bowl. Season to taste with salt and pepper. Let stand 30 minutes. Preheat broiler. Arrange oysters on broiler-proof pan. Spoon salsa over oysters, dividing evenly. Broil until heated through (about 5 minutes).

Roasted Oysters

6+ oysters in shells, per person
• garlic butter -- melted
• cocktail sauce
• fresh lemons
• rock salt
• pie pans or trays

The main ingredients for an oyster roast are: a hot charcoal fire, plenty of oysters, several sauces for dipping and ice cold beer. If roasting for a crowd you will need 1 grill for each couple.

Place oysters on grill racks over hot coals and cover with wet burlap sacks; steam for 20 minutes. This opens the shells slightly and makes it easier to pry open. After oysters have steamed, remove from grill and place on wood cutting board. Wearing heavy gloves, pry open oysters using an oyster knife. Discard top shell. At this point, spoon garlic butter over a few and place them back on grill until the "skirts ruffle". The remaining oysters can be eaten immediately sampling the other sauces. Pour rock salt into pie pans or trays and place oysters on top and serve, the salt will stabilize the shells in the pan. Serve with fresh bread for sopping up juices along with small bowls of warm garlic butter.

Cocktail Sauce

1 cup tomato ketchup
3 Tbsp. prepared white horseradish
1 Tbsp. Worcestershire sauce
• dash hot pepper sauce

Mix all ingredients together and refrigerate for 1 hour before serving.

15

Oyster Bienville

Serves 6 - 12

- 3 doz. oysters on the half shell
- 6 pie pans, covered with rock salt
- 4 Tbsp. butter
- ½ cup onion, minced
- ½ cup bell pepper, minced
- 1 cup scallions, minced
- 2 cloves garlic, minced
- 1½ cups raw shrimp, shelled & minced
- 1 cup fresh mushrooms, minced
- ½ cup white wine
- 1 Tbsp. fresh lemon juice
- 2 cups béchamel sauce (thick cream sauce)
- ⅔ cup grated Cheddar cheese
- ½ cup fresh French bread crumbs
- • salt, white pepper and hot pepper sauce to taste
- • dash of Angostura bitters

Preheat oven to 400° F.

Sauté the onion, bell pepper, green onions, mushrooms and garlic in butter until soft; add the shrimp and cook for 1 minute until barely pink. Deglaze with the white wine and lemon juice and bring to a boil. Add the béchamel sauce, cheese and bread crumbs and reduce to a simmer. Add salt, white pepper and pepper sauce to taste, dash bitters, then simmer for 20 minutes or until very thick.

Arrange 6 raw oysters in each of the salt lined pans. Cover each oyster with sauce and bake for 10 minutes, until the oysters and sauce are very hot and the top of the sauce is browned. Serve at once.

Oysters Lafitte

Serves 4

- 24 oysters on half shell
- • rock salt or sea salt

Garlic Cream Sauce
- 2 Tbsp. butter, clarified
- 1 clove garlic, minced
- 2 Tbsp. scallion, minced
- 1 tsp. dill weed
- 1 Tbsp. flour
- ½ cup white wine
- ½ cup heavy cream
- ½ lb. crab meat
- 2 Tbsp. butter, unsalted

Wine & Tarragon Sauce
- 2 large egg yolks, minced
- 1 tsp. fresh lemon juice
- 1 tsp. tarragon
- 2 Tbsp. white wine
- ½ lb. butter, clarified
- • salt to taste
- • white pepper to taste

Garlic Cream Sauce

Heat 2 tablespoons butter, garlic, scallions and dill in small skillet. Cook until vegetables are cooked but not browned. Stir in flour and add white wine and cream. Cook, stirring constantly until reduced and thickened. In another small pan, heat crabmeat in 2 tablespoons butter. Add heated crabmeat to cream sauce and keep warm.

Wine And Tarragon Sauce

Wisk together egg yolks, lemon juice, white wine and tarragon in medium saucepan. Carefully heat until mixture is reduced to a paste while continuing to whisk constantly. Remove hot paste from heat and slowly incorporate butter by whisking mixture while drizzling butter. Continue to whisk until sauce is thick and emulsified. Salt and pepper to taste.

Position oysters on a salt covered baking sheet and broil for 1 minute. Remove and spread with cream sauce and drizzle with wine sauce. Broil until browned and bubbly. Serve warm.

White Remoulade Sauce

2 cups homemade mayonnaise
1 clove garlic, finely chopped
4 scallions including some green tops, finely chopped
1 Tbsp. capers, drained & chopped
¼ cup sour gherkins, finely chopped
½ tsp. Worcestershire sauce
¼ tsp. cayenne pepper
¼ cup fresh parsley, finely chopped
3 anchovy fillets, mashed
½ lemon, juiced

In a bowl, whisk together all of the ingredients and chill for 1 hour before serving. Makes about 2½ cups.

Creamed Curry Oysters

Serves 2 - 4

24 oysters
3 scallions, minced
1 Tbsp. butter
1 cup white wine
• salt and white pepper to taste
1 cup heavy cream
2 tsp. curry powder
• minced scallions for garnish

In heavy skillet sauté 2 tablespoons scallions in butter until wilted. Add wine and pepper and bring to boil. Reduce heat to a simmer, cooking uncovered until reduced by half. Add cream while stirring over medium heat. Add curry and salt. Continue to cook until slightly thickened. Place 1 Tbsp. sauce over each oyster. Bake at 450° F for 3 minutes or until oysters begin to curl. Garnish with minced scallions.

N'awlins Oyster Fritters

Serves 8 - 12

1 qt. shucked oysters
6 eggs, beaten
4 Tbsp. baking powder
½ tsp. oregano
1 tsp. fresh ground pepper
½ tsp. white pepper
2 Tbsp. hot pepper sauce
2 cups all-purpose flour
1 cup half & half
1 Tbsp. salt
1 stick butter
• peanut or vegetable oil for frying

Drain oysters reserving liquid. In a large skillet over medium heat, sauté oysters in butter for 2 - 3 minutes. Remove oysters from pan and cool slightly. In large mixing bowl, mix eggs, half an half and hot pepper sauce together. In a separate bowl sift together the dry ingredients and slowly stir into egg mixture; forming a batter. Fold quartered oysters into batter and drop by tablespoonfuls into hot oil and fry until golden brown. If batter is too thick you can adjust its consistency with reserved liquid from oysters. Serve fritters hot with additional pepper sauce or dipping sauce.

17

Chicken & Oyster Gumbo

Serves 6

- 3 lb. chicken, cut into pieces
- 1 tsp. salt
- 1 tsp. fresh ground pepper
- 3 Tbsp. butter
- 1 Tbsp. vegetable oil
- ¼ cup all-purpose flour
- 2 large onions, chopped
- 2 celery stalks, chopped
- 1½ cups fresh okra, cleaned and sliced
- 3 cloves garlic, minced
- 3 cups chicken stock
- 1 cup water
- 1 Tbsp. Worcestershire sauce
- 1 Tbsp. dried red pepper flakes
- 1 bay leaf
- 1 tsp. fresh thyme, chopped
- ¼ tsp. ground allspice
- 24 shucked oysters
- ¼ cup fresh parsley, chopped
- 4 scallion tops, minced
- gumbo filé
- hot pepper sauce
- hot boiled rice

Sauté salt and peppered chicken pieces in oil and butter, in dutch oven, over medium heat. Once chicken is dark brown on all sides (about 20 minutes) remove from pan and set to the side. Lower heat and stir in flour. Cook, stirring frequently, until the roux turns dark brown (about 45 minutes). Be careful not to burn. Add onions, celery, okra and garlic. Stir roux and vegetables constantly while cooking for about 5 minutes. Add chicken stock, water, Worcestershire sauce, pepper flakes, bay leaf, thyme and allspice. After bringing to a boil, reduce heat and simmer uncovered for 30 minutes. Add chicken pieces and continue to simmer for 45 - 50 minutes. Add the oysters, parsley and scallion tops and cook 5 minutes longer. Remove bay leaf before serving over hot rice.

Basic Roux

- 1½ cups vegetable oil
- 2 cups all-purpose flour

Roux cannot be rushed; it is a gradual process and requires patience and attention. When roux is cooked too quickly it will brown but will not develop a good flavor. When done it may taste and smell slightly bitter. If you burn a roux, throw it out and start over.

Mix oil and flour in a heavy iron skillet. It should be like a soft batter; if not, add a little more oil. Cook over low to medium heat, stirring gently but constantly with a wooden spoon. As you stir be sure to lift mixture from bottom and sides of the skillet. If lumps develop, use a wire whisk until they break up. Cook until the color is nearly the color of chili powder. This will take from 30 - 60 minutes depending on the skillet being used. After the roux is done, remove from heat to cool, continuing to stir constantly for 3 - 4 minutes. Then stir frequently for about 10 minutes more. As it cools, oil with rise to the top; spoon it off. Place roux in a plastic or metal container and store in refrigerator until ready to use. Before using, skim any oil that has come to surface.

Let roux return to room temperature.

Serves 4

8	slices lean bacon, cut in 1-inch squares
28	medium sized fresh shucked oysters, drained
½	cup flour
½	tsp. cayenne
1	cup melted butter
¼	cup fresh lemon juice
4	long flat skewers

Linguini with Oyster Sauce

1	stick salted butter
½	cup olive oil
7	large cloves garlic, peeled and halved
1	tsp. dried basil
3	Tbsp. fresh parsley, minced
1	tsp. fresh ground pepper
2	Tbsp. salt
2	pints fresh shucked oysters, drained
4	quarts cold water
16	oz. linguini

Preheat broiler. Fry bacon squares partially (about 3 - 4 minutes). Drain on absorbent paper. Starting with a square of bacon, alternately place eight squares of bacon and seven oysters. Sprinkle with salt and pepper. Mix flour and cayenne and sprinkle evenly over the brochettes. Lay skewers across a broiler-safe pan. Rest ends of skewers on the edge so that oysters do not touch bottom and sides of pan. Combine melted butter and lemon juice. Drizzle about half of the lemon butter over the skewers and place about 4 inches from the broiler for about 3 minutes on each side. This should give them a lovely crisp crust. Remove from oven. Brush lightly with remaining sauce placing the remainder at the table when serving.

Linguini with Oyster Sauce: In sauté pan melt butter over low heat. Add ½ cup olive oil; mix well and heat for 2 minutes. Add garlic and sauté over medium heat for 4 minutes; don't let garlic brown. Remove garlic with slotted spoon. Add basil, parsley, pepper and ½ teaspoon salt; simmer for 4 minutes. Add the oysters and warm over low heat for 5 minutes. Remove sauce from heat, cover and set aside while preparing linguini. Combine water and 2 tablespoons of salt and 1 tablespoon olive oil in large stockpot and bring to a boil. Add linguini, when water comes to a boil again. Cook for 8 minutes.

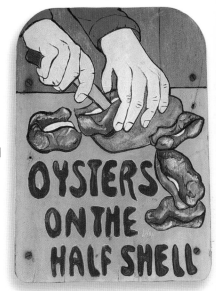

Drain linguini in colander and drain thoroughly. Return linguini to pot, add the oyster sauce and mix gently. Cover pot and place in 175˚ F oven for 5 minutes. When ready to serve toss mixture thoroughly.

Oysters in Sherry Cream

Serves 3 - 4

½	pint oysters, shucked
1	dash salt
1	dash black pepper
½	cup bread crumbs
2	Tbsp. butter, melted
1	Tbsp. dry sherry
½	cup half & half

Drain oysters and discard liquid. Place oysters in shallow baking dish (not glass) and sprinkle generously with salt and pepper. Combine bread crumbs with melted butter and distribute evenly over oysters. Mix sherry and half and half together and pour over breaded oysters. Place baking dish about 6" - 8" under broiler. Broil long enough to heat cream sauce and curl edges of the oysters (about 3 minutes). Serve immediately.

GLASSWARE

A. Collins   B. Highball   C. Old-Fashioned

D. Shot   E. Hurricane   F. Red Wine

G. White Wine   H. Cocktail

 A   B   C   D

 E   F   G    H

STANDARD BAR MEASURES:

		Standard	Metric
1	Dash (or splash)	1/32 oz.	0.9 ml.
1	Teaspoon	1/8 oz.	3.7 ml.
1	Tablespoon	3/8 oz.	11.1 ml.
1	Pony	1 oz.	29.5 ml.
1	Jigger	1½ oz.	44.5 ml.
1	Wineglass	4 oz.	119 ml.
1	Split	6 oz.	177 ml.
1	Cup	8 oz.	257 ml.

Pepper Mary

2 oz. vodka
6 oz. tomato juice
1 tsp. Worcestershire sauce
3-5 drops hot pepper sauce
• salt and pepper to taste
• pickle or celery stalk for garnish
• margarita salt

Moisten rim of glass and dip in mixture of margarita salt mixed with ground pepper. In shaker, mix vodka, tomato juice, Worcestershire and hot pepper sauce. Pour in dipped glass with ice. Garnish with pickle or celery stalk.

Lemon Drop Shooter

1½ oz. citron vodka
• cracked ice
• fresh lemon wedge
1 tsp. sugar

Generously coat lemon wedge with sugar. Briefly shake vodka with cracked ice to chill. Strain into shot glass. Drink vodka and chase by biting juice from sugar coated lemon wedge.

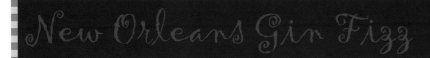

New Orleans Gin Fizz

Serves 1

1½ oz. dry gin
2 drops orange flower water
2 egg whites
5 tsp. powdered sugar
½ tsp. lemon juice
2 oz. half and half
1 drop vanilla extract
½ cup ice, coarsely chopped

Combine all the ingredients in an electric blender. Cover the blender and turn on high speed for 1½ minutes. (The mixture should become quite thick and airy, so blend some more if the mixture is too thin.) To serve, pour into a tall thin glass, or a double-sized old-fashioned glass.

Cajun Martini

2½ oz. pepper vodka
• splash dry vermouth

Coat martini glass with dry vermouth discarding excess. Shake pepper vodka quickly in ice. Pour off vodka into coated glass straining off ice. Garnish with a pepper stuffed olive.

23

Hurricane

2 oz. amber rum
¼ cup passion fruit juice
¼ cup pineapple juice
1 tsp. superfine sugar
½ tsp. grenadine
2 Tbsp. fresh lime juice
• ice cubes

Mix the rum, fruit juice and sugar until sugar is dissolved. Add grenadine and lime juice; stir to combine. Add ice cubes and shake. Strain hurricane into cocktail glass and garnish with orange slices and maraschino cherries.

Milk Punch

1½ oz. bourbon
2 oz. whole milk
2 oz. heavy cream
1 tsp. powdered sugar
1 drop vanilla extract
• cracked ice

Combine in cocktail shaker. Shake vigorously for 15 - 20 seconds. Strain punch into highball glass. Sprinkle lightly with nutmeg, if desired.

Oyster Shooter

Serves 6

6	raw oysters shucked and drained
2	Tbsp. unsalted butter
1	tsp. horseradish
2	tsp. pepper
1	2 jiggers vodka
1	lemon

Cut lemon into 6 wedges. In blender, combine tomato juice, horseradish and pepper. Mix thoroughly. Pour ½ shot of tomato juice mixture into a small glass. Add a shot of vodka. Put 1 raw oyster in the glass and garnish with lemon wedge. Bottoms up.

Sazerac

Serves 1

1	oz. bourbon or rye whiskey
2	drops Angostura bitters
2	drops Peychaud bitters
1	tsp. sugar syrup
1	tsp. Pernod
1	twist lemon peel

Combine all ingredients except the Pernod and lemon peel in a cocktail shaker. Put the Pernod into a chilled old-fashioned glass and then tilt the glass in all directions to thoroughly coat the inside with Pernod. Pour off any excess. Mix the ingredients in the shaker thoroughly with a cocktail spoon; do not shake. Strain into the chilled coated glass and place the twist of lemon peel on top.

Cosmopolitan Martini

1	oz. vodka
½	oz. orange liqueur
•	juice of ½ lime
•	splash of cranberry juice

Pour ingredients into container with ice. Shake several times and strain off into chilled martini glass.

26

Fried Soft Shell Crabs

Serves 4

- 4   large or 8 small soft shell crabs
- •   cold milk for soaking
- 2   cups all-purpose flour
- 1   tsp. salt
- ½   tsp. freshly ground pepper
- ¼   tsp. cayenne
- •   vegetable oil for deep-frying

To clean the crabs: Lay them, back down, on paper towels spread out on a cutting board. Remove the loose triangular covering on the underside of the crabs and then turn them over. With a very sharp knife cut off about ⅓-inch of the front of the head. This will remove the eyes. Reach into the opening and remove the small gray sac that is behind the eye cavity. Lift up the point flaps on each side of the top and pull out the fibrous matter with your fingers. Lay the flaps down again. Be careful when handling these delicate crabs.

To fry: Rinse the cleaned crabs under cold water and gently pat dry. Soak in cold milk for 15 minutes. Add seasonings to the flour and mix well. Heat oil to 375° F. Remove crabs from milk and let drain. Roll crabs gently in flour to coat and place on rack over baking sheet. Fry crabs one or two at a time, 6 - 12 minutes, depending on size. Carefully turn crabs with tongs during frying to brown evenly. Remove crabs and let oil drain. Place on a paper towel lined platter and insert into a 200° F oven while the remaining crabs are being prepared.

Beer Boiled Crab

Serves 6

- 6   medium hard-shelled crabs
- 2   tsp. salt
- 1   tsp. fresh ground black pepper
- 1   tsp. sesame oil
- 1   Tbsp. oyster sauce
- 3   garlic cloves, thin sliced
- 1   large onion, sliced
- 2   Tbsp. vegetable oil
- 2   small fresh red chiles, sliced
- 12   oz. beer
- 2   medium Cajun tomatoes, peeled and diced
- 3   scallions, sliced

Marinate crabs in salt, pepper, sesame oil, oyster sauce and 1 clove of garlic for 1 hour. In large skillet, sauté onion and remaining garlic in vegetable oil until vegetables begin to brown. Remove crabs from marinade. Add crabs and chile slices to skillet. Pour in beer and cover skillet. Bring to low boil and cook crabs for 10 minutes. Add tomatoes and return to low boil for 5 minutes longer. Serve in bowls with a little broth and garnish with sliced scallions. Serve with hot bread.

Crab Stuffed Eggplant

Serves 4

2	medium eggplants
4	Tbsp. butter (divided)
2	large cloves garlic, crushed
1	cup scallions, chopped
1	cup celery, sliced
½	cup red bell pepper, finely chopped
½	cup parsley, finely chopped
1½	cups soft French bread crumbs, divided
2	tsp. fresh thyme, chopped
1	tsp. fresh rosemary, chopped
1	Tbsp. fresh oregano, chopped
1	Tbsp. fresh basil, chopped
2	eggs, slightly beaten
1	tsp. salt
½	tsp. black pepper
⅛	tsp. hot pepper sauce
1	lb. crabmeat
1	large lemon, juiced
½	cup Romano cheese, freshly grated
•	chopped parsley

Wash and dry eggplants. Preheat oven to 350° F. Place eggplants on a baking pan and bake about 35 or 40 minutes or just until tender. Remove from oven, cut in half lengthwise and cool. With a spoon or sharp knife, scoop out pulp, leaving a ½-inch shell. Chop or mash pulp. While eggplants are baking, sauté garlic, scallions, celery and bell pepper in 2 tablespoons butter until soft but not browned. Remove from heat and combine with eggplant pulp and all remaining ingredients except ½ cup breadcrumbs, remaining butter and cheese. Mix lightly and taste to correct seasonings. Spoon filling loosely into reserved eggplant shells. Top with remaining breadcrumbs and dot with remaining butter. Arrange filled shells on an oiled shallow pan; do not crowd. Preheat oven to 350° F and bake about 20 - 25 minutes or until hot and lightly browned. During the last 5 - 6 minutes, sprinkle with cheese. Serve garnished with chopped parsley. This filling may also be baked in a buttered casserole dish instead of eggplant shells.

Crab-Stuffed Mushrooms

Serves 6 - 8

1	lb. fresh mushrooms
2	Tbsp. onion, chopped
2	Tbsp. butter, salted
¼	cup soft bread cubes
¼	cup crabmeat, chopped
½	tsp. salt
2	tsp. lemon juice
¼	tsp. Worcestershire sauce
⅓	cup vermouth
½	cup sharp Cheddar cheese, shredded

Clean mushrooms, separating caps from stems. Chop stems and place in small skillet with butter and onion. Sauté vegetables until tender. Add crabmeat and bread cubes and cook over medium heat until lightly browned. Remove from heat and stir in salt, lemon juice and Worcestershire sauce. Fill mushroom caps with crabmeat mixture and arrange stuffed mushrooms in shallow baking dish. Pour vermouth around mushroom caps. Place in a 400° F. preheated oven and bake for 15 minutes. Top caps with cheese and continue to bake for another 6 minutes, until cheese is melted.

Crab Cakes

Serves 4

- 4 Tbsp. butter
- ¾ cup onion, finely chopped
- ¼ cup green bell pepper, finely chopped
- ¼ cup red bell pepper, finely chopped
- ¼ cup celery, finely chopped
- 3 egg yolks
- 1 whole egg
- ¼ cup mayonnaise
- 2 tsp. lemon juice
- 2 tsp. salt
- 1 tsp. mustard powder
- 6 dashes hot pepper sauce
- 1 tsp. Creole seasoning
- 1 cup fresh bread crumbs
- 1 lb. crabmeat

Melt butter in a skillet and sauté onion, peppers and celery just until tender. Transfer to a mixing bowl.

Combine egg yolks, whole egg and mayonnaise and beat well. Beat in vinegar, lemon juice, seasonings and parsley. Mix in breadcrumbs and fold in crabmeat.

Divide into equal portions and shape into cakes. Dust with flour and sauté in hot oil or butter, turning to brown both sides. (For a first course, make small crab cakes and allow two per serving.)

Marinated Party Shrimp

Serves 2 - 4

- 3 lbs. raw shrimp
- 1 bag shrimp boil
- 1 Tbsp. liquid shrimp boil
- 2 cups sliced onions
- 2 Tbsp. capers with juice
- 2 tsp. celery seed
- 8 bay leaves
- 1¼ cup oil
- ¾ cup vinegar
- 8 dashes hot pepper sauce

In large pot filled ¾ with water, bring shrimp boil seasonings and salt to a rolling boil. Add shrimp and boil just until pink; do not overcook. Drain, shell and devein shrimp. In a large plastic or glass container, layer shrimp, onion slices, bay leaves and capers. In a separate bowl, combine remaining ingredients. Pour over shrimp and cover. Refrigerate for 24 hours, while shaking or stirring every few hours. Discard marinade and bay leaves before serving.

Louie Sauce

- 1 cup mayonnaise
- ½ cup whipping cream, whipped
- ¼ cup chili sauce
- 2 Tbsp. onion minced
- • salt and pepper to taste

Mix all ingredients together and chill at least 1 hour before serving.

Chicken Andouille over Dirty Rice

Serves 8

1	3 lb. fryer, cut up
½	cup seasoned flour to coat chicken
3	Tbsp. vegetable oil
¼	cup all-purpose flour
½	lb. chicken gizzards, cooked and minced
½	lb. lean boneless pork, cooked and crumbled
2	onions, chopped
1	stalk celery, chopped
1	small green bell pepper, seeded and chopped
1	small red bell pepper, seeded and chopped
2	cloves garlic, minced
¼	lb. chicken livers cooked, and minced
6	green onions, chopped
1½	cups chicken stock
1	tsp. salt
¼	tsp. ground pepper
½	tsp. hot pepper sauce
8	cups hot cooked long-grain rice
2	Tbsp. fresh parsley, chopped
2	lbs. andouille sausage, sliced into bite size pieces

Dust chicken pieces with seasoned flour and fry for 20 - 25 minutes in oil, over medium heat. When done, remove chicken and keep in warm oven until ready to use. Whisk flour in the chicken drippings (if mixture is as thick as pudding, add a little more oil to thin). Cook, stirring frequently, over low heat until the roux is the color of dark mahogany (about 25 minutes). Do not let the roux burn. Add the gizzards, pork, onions, celery, peppers and garlic. Cook, stirring occasionally, 15 minutes longer. Remove from heat and add the rice and green onions, salt, pepper, hot pepper sauce and andouille slices. Spread rice mixture in a large baking dish. Place chicken on top of rice and cover. Bake in 350° F preheated oven for 20 minutes or until heated through. Serve immediately.

Creole Crocked Chicken

Serves 6

1½	lbs. boneless chicken breasts
2	cloves garlic, crushed
6	lrg. tomatoes, skinned and chopped
2	large onions, chopped
1	large bell pepper, chopped
¼	cup Worcestershire sauce
¼	cup soy sauce, reduced sodium
2	tsp. fresh ground pepper
2	Tbsp. fresh basil, chopped
2	Tbsp. fresh marjoram, chopped
1	Tbsp. fresh oregano, chopped
•	hot steamed rice

Sauté chicken pieces and garlic in large skillet until chicken is cooked through. Stir in Worcestershire sauce and soy sauce. Place chicken mixture in slow cooker or crock pot and turn on low heat. Add herbs and vegetables, topping off with diced tomatoes. Cover and allow to cook slowly for 4 - 6 hours. Serve over hot rice.

Red Beans & Rice

Serves 4

1	lb.	dry red beans
6	cups	cold water
6	cups	hot water
1	lb.	ham hocks
2		bay leaves
3	cups	onion, chopped
1	cup	celery, chopped
½	cup	sliced green onions
1	Tbsp.	salt
1	tsp.	ground pepper
¼	tsp.	dried thyme
1	tsp.	cayenne
1	lb.	andouille sausage

Rice

3	quarts	salted water
1	Tbsp.	vegetable oil
1	Tbsp.	vinegar

Rinse beans. In a Dutch oven, cover the beans with 6 cups cold water. Bring to a boil. Reduce heat and simmer 3 minutes. Remove from heat. Cover and let stand 1 hour. Drain and rinse. Return beans to Dutch oven; add 6 cups hot water, ham hocks and bay leaves. Cook over low heat for 2 hours. Add onion, celery, green onion, salt, pepper and dried thyme. Cook over low heat for 1 to 1½ hours more. Slice sausage into bite-size pieces and sauté for 15 minutes or until heated through. Add sausage to beans about 30 minutes before serving. Be sure beans are fresh; they will be tender and become creamy during the cooking process. Old beans will never be tender.

Bring salted water to a rapid boil. Add oil and vinegar. Slowly add 1 cup of long grain rice that has not been rinsed but inspected for stones. Reduce heat and simmer for 18 minutes. Drain rice and rinse. Steam in colander over hot water to warm before serving.

Louisiana Meatloaf

Serves 6

¾	cup	onion, finely chopped
½	cup	celery, finely chopped
½	cup	bell pepper, finely chopped
¼	cup	scallions, finely chopped
2		hot banana peppers, finely chopped
3		cloves garlic, minced
1	Tbsp.	hot pepper sauce
1	Tbsp.	Worcestershire sauce
½	cup	evaporated milk
¼	cup	ketchup
¼	cup	tomato sauce
1½	lb.	lean ground beef
½	lb.	ground pork
2		eggs, beaten
1	cup	bread crumbs, fine
4	Tbsp.	butter
1	tsp.	salt
1	tsp.	fresh ground pepper
1	tsp.	cayenne pepper
½	tsp.	white pepper
1	tsp.	cumino, ground
½	tsp.	nutmeg, ground
2		bay leaves

Heat butter, onions, celery, peppers, garlic and scallions in medium sauce-pan until vegetables are tender. Add dry seasonings, hot pepper sauce and Worcestershire sauce to vegetable mixture and continue to cook until mixture begins to stick excessively to pan. Add milk, ketchup and tomato sauce, stirring until well incorporated. Remove from heat and allow to cool to room temperature. Once cooled remove and discard bay leaves. In large mixing bowl, mix ground beef, ground pork, eggs, bread crumbs and seasoning mixture. Preheat oven to 350° F. Place mixed meat mixture into 13" X 9" baking dish and form into loaf 2" tall, 5" wide and 12" long. Place in preheated oven for 30 minutes. Increase oven temperature to 400° F and continue to bake until loaf reaches an internal temperature of 165° F. Remove from oven and allow to rest for 15 minutes. Slice and serve.

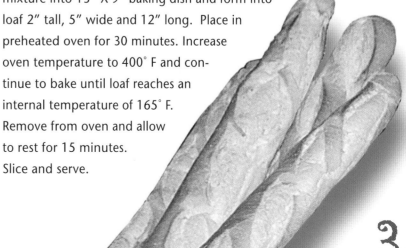

Roast Pork Loin

Serves 4 - 6

3-5 lb. pork loin with ribs intact
¼ cup olive oil
¼ cup fresh rosemary, chopped

Horseradish Sauce

¼ cup prepared white horseradish
2 Tbsp. Creole mustard
2 Tbsp. white vinegar
¼ tsp. white pepper
¼ tsp. sugar
½ cup heavy cream

Brush raw roast with olive oil. Rub with rosemary and fresh black pepper. Place fat side up on a rack in uncovered roasting pan. Roast at 375° F and check after one hour. Roast to an internal temperature of 180° F and remove roast to a warmed platter to rest for 15 minutes before slicing. While roast is in the oven, prepare the sauce. To make the sauce, combine all the ingredients except the cream. Allow to stand at room temperature for 15 minutes. Briskly whisk sauce while slowly adding the heavy cream. Cover the dish and refrigerate until ready to serve the roast.

Andouille Black Bean Stew

Serves 6 - 8

2 cups black turtle beans
6 cups water
1 lb. andouille sausage, grilled and cut into ½" pieces
3 red potatoes, cubed with peel
½ cup carrots, sliced ¼"
¼ cup celery, sliced ¼"
1 medium onion, chopped
5 cups light chicken broth
1 cup beef broth
12 oz. beer
1 bay leaf
¼ tsp. cayenne
2 tsp. Creole seasoning
1 Tbsp. white wine vinegar
3 Tbsp. parsley, chopped
• hot pepper sauce, to taste

Wash and sort beans in cold water, removing any stones or debris. Place washed beans and water in 5-quart Dutch oven. Heat over medium heat until pot begins to boil. Cover and simmer for 15 minutes. Remove from heat and drain. Add chicken and beef broth and stir in potatoes, carrots, celery, onions, beer and bay leaf. Return to heat and simmer for another 10 minutes, stirring occasionally. Preheat oven to 275° F. Remove from heat and add andouille sausage, cayenne and Creole seasoning. Mix thoroughly. Place covered Dutch oven in pre-heated oven for 1½ to 2 hours or until beans are tender. Remove from oven and stir in vinegar and desired amount of hot pepper sauce and chopped parsley. Serve in bowls with fresh hot French bread.

Cajun Seafood Jambalaya

Serves 4

2	Tbsp. salted butter
4	cups onion, chopped
⅔	cup green pepper, chopped
⅓	cup green scallion tops, thinly sliced
1	Tbsp. garlic, minced
2	Tbsp. parsley, minced
2	cups baked ham, finely chopped
1	lb. pork, ¾" cubes
6	smoked sausages
1½	lbs. shrimp, peeled and deveined
1½	cups long-grain rice
3	cups rich beef stock
2½	tsp. salt
¼	tsp. black pepper, freshly ground
⅛	tsp. cayenne pepper
½	tsp. chili powder
2	whole bay leaves
¼	tsp. dried thyme
⅛	tsp. cloves

In a heavy 7 - 8 quart pot or kettle, melt the butter over low heat. Add the vegetables, parsley, pork and ham. Continue to cook over low heat, stirring constantly, for about 15 minutes or until the vegetables and pieces of meat are browned. Add the sausage and seasonings and continue cooking and stirring over low heat for 5 minutes more. Add the rice, beef stock and shrimp, mixing well. Raise the heat to high and bring to a boil. Cover the pot and turn the heat to very low. Cook for 45 minutes, uncovering from time to time to stir. Uncover the pot during the last 10 minutes of cooking and raise the heat to medium. Stir gently and frequently as the rice dries out. Serve immediately.

Chicken Jambalaya

Serves 6 - 8

2	Tbsp. vegetable oil
1	3 - 4 lbs. frying chicken, cut up, rinsed & dried
4	cups onion, chopped
¾	cup green pepper, chopped
¾	cup green scallion tops, sliced thinly
1	Tbsp. garlic, minced
3	Tbsp. parsley, finely minced
½	cup lean baked ham, finely chopped
1	lb. lean pork, ½" cubes
6	sausages-Creole, Polish or French Garlic, ½" slices
½	tsp. pepper, freshly ground
¼	tsp. cayenne pepper
½	tsp. chili powder
2	whole bay leaves, crushed
¼	tsp. dried thyme
⅛	tsp. cloves
¼	tsp. dried basil
⅛	tsp. mace
1½	cups long-grain white rice
3	cups water

In a heavy 7 to 8 quart pot or kettle, heat the oil over high heat. Brown the chicken parts in the hot oil, turning them frequently with long-handled tongs to ensure even browning. As the pieces brown, remove them to a large platter. When all the chicken is browned and removed, add the vegetables, parsley, ham and pork to the pot. Reduce the heat to medium and cook, stirring frequently, for about 15 minutes, or until the vegetables and pieces of meat are browned. Add the sausage and seasonings and continue cooking and stirring for 5 minutes more, then add the reserved chicken parts, rice and water. Mix gently. Raise the heat to high and bring to a boil, then cover the pot and turn the heat to very low. Cook for 45 minutes, uncovering from time to time to stir. Uncover the pot during the last 10 minutes of cooking and raise the heat to medium. Stir gently and frequently as the rice dries out. Serve immediately.

39

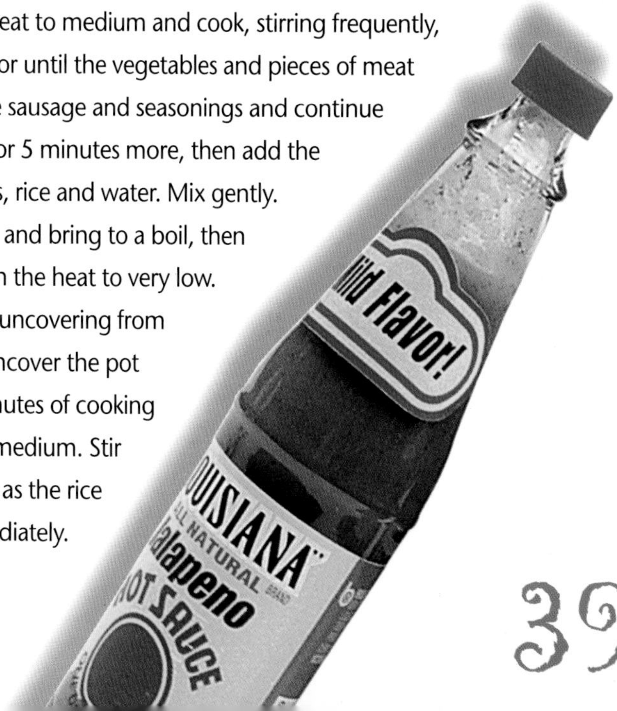

Barbeque Shrimp

Serves 2 - 4

2	sticks butter
1	cup vegetable oil
3	tsp. garlic, finely minced
4	whole bay leaves, crushed fine
2	tsp. dried rosemary, crushed
½	tsp. dried basil
½	tsp. oregano
½	tsp. salt
½	tsp. cayenne pepper
1	Tbsp. hot pepper sauce
¾	tsp. fresh ground pepper
1	tsp. fresh lemon juice
2	lb. whole fresh shrimp in the shell

In a saucepan melt the butter, add the oil and mix well. Add remaining ingredients, except shrimp. Cook over medium heat, stirring constantly, until sauce begins to boil. Reduce heat and simmer for 10 minutes, stirring frequently. Remove from heat and let rest at room temperature for 30 minutes. Add the shrimp and toss to coat thoroughly. Cook over medium heat for 5 - 8 minutes, or until shrimp just begins to turn pink. Remove from heat and place in preheated 450° F oven and bake for 10 minutes. Divide shrimp in equal portions into soup bowls and ladle the sauce over each portion. No need for knives or forks—just plenty of napkins and crusty French bread for dipping.

Bacon-Wrapped Shrimp Skewers

Serves 6

36	large raw shrimp, peeled and deveined
12	thick bacon slices
18	slices fresh jalapeño
6	oz. monterey jack cheese
2	tsp. salt
2	tsp. paprika
1	tsp. Cajun seasoning
¼	tsp. cayenne
6	wooden or metal skewers

Partially cook bacon slices over medium heat, without browning. Slices need to still be flexible enough to wrap easily around shrimp. Cut slits down the back of shrimp, about halfway, to make a pocket for jalapeño and cheese. Bring 4 cups water to boil in medium saucepan. Drop in shrimp and jalapeño slices and cook for 1 minute. Remove immediately and rinse with cold water. You do not want the shrimp cooked completely. Drain shrimp and jalapeños thoroughly. Cut jalapeño slices in half and remove seeds. Assemble skewers by inserting jalapeño crescent and jack cheese into pocket in shrimp. Starting over the cheese, wrap with bacon 1½ times. Slide wrapped shrimp onto skewer in such a way as to hold bacon. Each skewer should hold 5 - 6 shrimp. Place skewers on broiler pan and lightly sprinkle with seasonings. Broil 3 - 4 minutes or until bacon begins to brown and cheese begins to melt.

Shrimp Bordeaux

Serves 3 - 4

½	lb. raw shrimp, peeled and deveined
1	large potato, cooked and diced
4	Tbsp. butter, salted
1	tsp. white pepper
½	tsp. cayenne
½	lb. fresh mushrooms, sliced
1	medium onion, diced
1	cup artichoke hearts, quartered
1	cup sugar snap peas
2	Tbsp. fresh chives, chopped
2	Tbsp. salt
¼	cup white wine

Clean and prepare vegetables. Melt butter in 12" skillet. Add white pepper, cayenne, mushrooms and onions and sauté over medium heat until vegetables are crispy tender. Stir in snap peas and chives, along with shrimp, artichoke hearts and cubed potatoes. Add white wine and salt to taste. Continue to heat, stirring occasionally until shrimp are cooked bright pink and vegetables are heated through.

42

Shrimp & Leek Pizza

Serves 2

1	Tbsp. olive oil
2	tsp. dried red pepper flakes
½	cup fontina cheese
1	cup fresh mozzerella cheese, sliced
12	prawns or jumbo shrimp, rinsed and peeled
2	plum or Creole tomatoes, thinly sliced
1	small leek
4	cloves garlic, thinly sliced
¼	fresh basil, chopped

Preheat oven to 500° F. Butterfly and devein the shrimp and set aside. Clean and dry leek, slice white portion and discard the green top. Work dough as directed in pizza dough recipe. Brush dough with olive oil and sprinkle with chile pepper flakes. Top dough with half of the following, in order; cheeses, basil, tomatoes, leek, shrimp and garlic. Slide pizza onto hot stone and bake for 10 - 12 minutes.

Grilled Creole Shrimp

Serves 2 - 4

2	lbs. jumbo raw shrimp
8	cloves garlic
4	scallions
¼	cup fresh oregano
2	Tbsp. fresh thyme
1	cup butter, softened
1	Tbsp. Worcestershire sauce
1	tsp. salt
1	tsp. fresh ground pepper
3	dashes hot pepper sauce
2	lemons, cut in wedges

Snip along back of shrimp, with small sharp scissors and remove vein. Rinse shrimp, leaving shell on. In food processor mince garlic, scallions, oregano and thyme. Add butter, Worcestershire sauce, salt and peppers. Blend herbs and spices into butter. Scrape sides of bowl to insure spices are well incorporated. Work a small amount of Creole butter between the shrimp and its shell. Refrigerate buttered shrimp for up to eight hours. To cook, brush grill with oil and place shrimp over medium coals. Grill until shrimp turn pink on bottom side. Turn shrimp over and continue to cook until shrimp is fully pink and flesh is opaque in appearance (about 6 - 8 minutes). Serve immediately with lemon wedges and plenty of napkins.

Louisiana Shrimp

Serves 4 - 6

1	lb. large shrimp, peeled and deveined
3	Tbsp. butter
½	cup onion, chopped
1	cup mushrooms, sliced
¼	cup white wine
1	Tbsp. cornstarch
1	tsp. salt
1	tsp. Worcestershire Sauce
½	tsp. cayenne
2	Tbsp. fresh parsley, chopped

Melt butter in large heavy skillet. Add chopped onion and sliced mushrooms. Sauté over medium heat until onions are transparent. Add shrimp and continue to cook, while stirring. Combine remaining ingredients and stir into shrimp mixture. Cook only until sauce thickens. Toss in parsley and serve immediately over noodles or steamed rice.

Shrimp Étoufeé

Serves 4

6 Tbsp. salted butter
¼ cup all-purpose flour
1 cup onion, chopped
½ cup celery, chopped
½ cup green pepper, chopped
1 Tbsp. garlic, finely minced
2 cups shrimp, peeled & deveined
1 tsp. salt
¼ tsp. fresh ground pepper
¼ tsp. cayenne
1 tsp. fresh lemon juice
½ cup green onion, thinly sliced
1 cup cold water
2 cups hot water
• boiled rice

Melt butter in Dutch oven over low heat. Gradually add the flour, stirring constantly. Cook over low heat until a medium brown roux is formed (approximately 15 minutes). Add the onion, green pepper, celery and garlic; continue to cook, stirring often, until vegetables are tender (about 20 minutes). Add the shrimp, salt, pepper, cayenne, lemon juice and green onions. Mix well. Add the cold water and bring to a boil. Lower heat and simmer for 10 minutes, stirring often, until shrimp turns pink. Remove from heat. Prepare rice. Before serving, slowly heat over low heat, gradually adding 1 - 2 cups hot water to create gravy. Serve over boiled rice.

Shrimp Rémoulade

Serves 4

1 scallion, chopped
1 Tbsp. celery, chopped
2 Tbsp. fresh parsley, minced
4 cups romaine lettuce, coarsely chopped
1 lb. whole fresh shrimp, boiled, chilled, peeled and deveined

Rémoulade Sauce

1 bunch scallions, sliced
2 small stalks celery, chopped
2 sprigs fresh parsley, minced
3 Tbsp. Creole mustard
5 tsp. paprika
1¼ tsp. salt
½ tsp. black pepper, freshly ground
¼ tsp. cayenne
6 Tbsp. white wine vinegar
5 tsp. fresh lemon juice
½ tsp. dried basil
¾ cup olive oil

Grind the bunch of scallions, celery stalks and parsley sprigs in a food mill or reduce almost to a purée in an electric blender. Place the vegetable puree in a china or stainless steel bowl. Add the mustard, paprika, salt, pepper and cayenne and blend with a wire whisk. Add the vinegar, lemon juice and basil, blending again. Gradually add the olive oil, stirring constantly. When well blended, add the chopped scallions, chopped celery and the finely minced parsley and stir with wooden spoon to mix thoroughly. Cover the bowl with plastic wrap and refrigerate for at least 3 hours. At serving time, chop the lettuce and put 1 cup on each salad plate. Place the boiled shrimp on top of the lettuce, and after stirring it well, pour about ¼ cup rémoulade sauce over each portion. The sauce should completely cover shrimp. Serve well chilled.

Gaspergou

Serves 4 - 6

1   whole redfish, split and cleaned
½   cup water
12   slices lemon, about ⅛" thick

Sauce
¼   cup salted butter
¼   cup olive oil
¼   cup all-purpose flour
3   small onions, peeled and sliced ⅛"
¾   cup scallion tops, sliced
2   cloves garlic, minced
¼   cup fresh parsley, chopped
⅓   cup green bell pepper, chopped
1   large can peeled whole tomatoes,
      coarsely chopped
1½   cup fish stock
3   bay leaves
1   tsp. thyme
1½   tsp. dried basil
¼   cup fresh lemon juice
2   tsp. salt

Preheat oven to 375° F. Melt butter and olive oil in large skillet over low heat. Add flour and continue to cook while stirring frequently, until a golden brown roux forms. Quickly add the onions, scallions, garlic, parsley and bell pepper. Cook just until the vegetables become tender. Remove from heat and stir in tomatoes, water and remaining sauce ingredients. Pour sauce into a large baking dish, about 3" deep and long enough to hold your fish. Cut the cleaned fish into steaks, starting just below the head. Continue with the 2" steaks making sure to keep them in order. Reassemble the steaks over the sauce until the fish appears to be whole again. Arrange lemon slices on top of the fish. Place in oven and bake for 20 - 35 minutes. Bake until the fish steaks flake easily. Serve steaks with the sauce and a lemon slice.

Peppered Catfish with Chanterelles

Serves 4

2   10-oz. catfish fillets
2   tsp. cracked black pepper
3   Tbsp. olive oil
3   thick slices bacon, cooked and crumbled
1   cup Chanterelle mushrooms
1   medium onion, halved and thinly sliced
½   cup pecan halves
2   scallions, sliced
2   cloves garlic, crushed
•   juice from ½ lemon
1   tsp. fresh parsley, chopped
1   tsp. fresh basil leaves, chopped
½   tsp. fresh thyme
•   salt to taste

Preheat oven to 325° F. Cut each fillet into 2 portions. Season with cracked black pepper and lightly with salt. Heat olive oil in medium skillet over medium-high heat. When oil just begins to smoke add fish fillets and sear for 2 minutes on each side. Remove fish and place fillets in baking dish and bake until fish is done (about 6 minutes).

Return skillet to flame and lower heat slightly. Add onions and mushrooms to skillet and sauté for 3 - 4 minutes or until onions begin to become translucent. Add scallions, garlic, pecans and herbs to skillet and continue to sauté until herbs are wilted. Place mushroom onion mixture on warmed plates. Top with catfish fillet. Fresh sweet potato compliments this dish nicely. Other mushrooms may be used if Chanterelles are not available.

47

Grilled Red Snapper

Serves 4

4	small redfish butterflied
•	salt
•	cayenne pepper
½	cup butter, melted
1	lemon, juiced

Season fish generously with salt and cayenne pepper. Combine butter and lemon juice. Place the fish scales down, directly on the grill over a medium fire. Baste generously with butter and lemon mixture. Cover grill and cook from 7 - 10 minutes or until fish flake.

Tilapia with Mango Salsa

Serves 4

4	tilapia fillets
1	Tbsp. olive oil
2	large tomatoes, peeled and chopped
8	scallions, finely chopped
2	cloves garlic, crushed
1	fresh jalapeño, seeded and finely chopped
1	fresh ripe mango, chopped
•	juice from ½ lime
2	Tbsp. ripe olives, sliced
2	Tbsp. tequila
2	Tbsp. fresh cilantro, chopped
•	steamed rice

Preheat oven to 350° F. Season fish fillets with salt and pepper and place on a greased baking sheet. Place fillets in oven and bake until done. Flesh will flake easily when tested. While fish is baking, prepare salsa by heating olive oil in medium skillet. Over medium-high heat, sauté tomatoes, green onions, garlic and jalapeño for 1 - 2 minutes. Add mango, lime juice, ripe olives and tequila. Lower heat to medium and continue to heat salsa for another 2 - 3 minutes. Toss in cilantro. Serve fish covered with salsa over steamed rice.

Redfish with Tomato Artichoke Sauce

Serves 6

6	8-oz. redfish fillets
2	Tbsp. virgin olive oil
4	cloves garlic, minced
2½	cups crushed roma tomatoes in purée
½	cup red wine
1	Tbsp. fresh rosemary, chopped
2	tsp. salt
½	tsp. fresh ground pepper
½	tsp. cayenne
1½	cups artichoke hearts, quartered
2	Tbsp. fresh parsley chopped
2	Tbsp. capers
2	Tbsp. fresh basil, chopped

In large skillet sauté olive oil and garlic (about 1 minute) over medium heat. Stir in tomatoes, red wine, rosemary, salt and peppers. Bring to a slow boil and reduce heat. Cover sauce and simmer for 15 minutes while stirring occasionally. Season redfish fillet with salt and pepper and gently place into sauce. Cover skillet and continue to simmer for 6 - 8 minutes or just until fish is done. Carefully remove fish from sauce and place on platter of hot buttered pasta. Increase heat to sauce and add artichoke hearts and parsley. Stir sauce until heated through. Spoon sauce over fish and pasta and garnish with capers and fresh basil.

Pompano Packets

Serves 4

4	pompano or red fish fillets
•	paprika
•	salt
•	fresh ground pepper
2	tsp. fresh rosemary or fresh oregano, finely chopped
2	small onions, thinly sliced
8	large black olives, thinly sliced
½	red bell pepper, thinly sliced
4	tsp. fresh lemon juice
8	Tbsp. olive oil or melted butter
•	parchment paper

Cut 4 parchment paper hearts 12" long and 8" wide. Oil parchment hearts well. Place fillets on oiled hearts. Season with salt and ground pepper and a liberal sprinkling of paprika. Sprinkle ½ teaspoon of rosemary or oregano on each fillet and top with pepper, onion and olive slices. Sprinkle 1 teaspoon of lemon juice and 2 tablespoons olive oil over each fillet. Seal edges of hearts by folding up edges and pinching closed. Grill over hot coals for about 10 minutes. Cooking time will vary with thickness of fillet. Transfer the packets to plates. Open packets at the table with a sharp knife.

Snapper Pernod

Serves 6

6	8-oz. snapper fillets
2	Tbsp. butter
2	scallions, minced
1	cup mushrooms, sliced
2	cups fish stock
½	cup white wine
1	cup heavy cream
¼	tsp. white pepper
¼	cup Pernod
4	Tbsp. butter
•	salt to taste

Sauté mushrooms and scallions in butter using a large heavy skillet over medium heat (about 5 minutes). Add fish stock and white wine and bring to boil. Add fish fillets, lowering heat to simmer until fish is near done and begins to flake when tested. Using slotted spatula or spoon, carefully transfer fish and mushrooms to heated platter and keep warm. Increase heat to high and reduce liquid by half. Add heavy cream and white pepper and reduce by half again, while stirring. Lower heat and add Pernod and butter chips, whisking until blended. Salt sauce to taste and pour sauce over fish. This is a great dish served with steamed vegetables and rice pilau.

Cajun Popcorn

1	egg, beaten
1	cup ice water
1	Tbsp. dry white wine
1	Tbsp. Creole seasoning
1	cup cake flour
•	crawfish tails
•	oil for deep frying

Beat the egg and mix with the water and white wine. Add flour and Creole seasoning and mix until thin batter is formed. Working in batches of 6 - 10 pieces, dip crawfish tails in batter, letting excess drip off. Drop in hot oil, piece by piece and keep turning until "popcorn" turns golden brown. Drain on absorbent paper and serve with splashes of hot pepper sauce.

51

Creole Catfish with Okra Medley

Serves 4

- 4 catfish fillets
- 1 Tbsp. paprika
- 3 Tbsp. Creole seasonings
- 1 tsp. salt
- ½ tsp. fresh ground pepper
- 2 tsp. fresh parsley, chopped
- 1 med. onion, chopped
- 12 med. okra, sliced
- 12 large black olives, quartered
- 2 plum tomatoes, seeded and chopped
- 1 clove garlic, minced
- 4 dashes hot pepper sauce
- 2 Tbsp. olive oil
- 1 lemon

Preheat oven to 375° F. In pestle or mill combine the paprika, Creole seasoning, salt and pepper. Sprinkle spice mixture generously on both sides of fillets. Spray baking dish with vegetable spray. Arrange fillets closely, but just barely touching. In medium bowl, combine parsley, onion, okra, black olives, tomatoes, garlic and hot pepper sauce. Generously spoon medley over the fish. Drizzle with olive oil and lemon juice. Bake uncovered for 15 - 20 minutes or until fish flakes easily.

Sea Bass with Creamy Pesto Topping

Serves 6

- 6 6-oz. sea bass or roughy fillets
- 1 tsp. salt
- ½ tsp. fresh ground pepper
- ½ tsp. paprika
- ¼ tsp. garlic powder
- ¼ tsp. onion powder

Topping:

- 4 Tbsp. salted butter
- ½ cup onion, finely chopped
- 1 bunch scallions, chopped
- 20 oz. frozen chopped spinach
- 2 tsp. salt
- ¼ tsp. ground nutmeg
- 6 oz. cream cheese
- ½ cup pine nuts
- 2 tsp. grated lemon peel
- ½ cup parmesan cheese
- • lemon slices

Preheat oven to 375° F. Thaw spinach and squeeze lightly to remove excess water and set aside. Place fish fillets in large flat buttered baking dish. Sprinkle salt, pepper, paprika, garlic and onion powder over fillets. Place spinach in a microwavable dish with lid. Microwave spinach on high heat, for 5 - 6 minutes or follow package directions. In skillet, over medium heat, sauté butter and pine nuts together, until nuts begin to brown. Add onions and continue to cook until onions become transparent. Lower heat and stir in salt, nutmeg and ground pepper. Add cooked spinach to onions and nuts. Remove from heat and stir in cream cheese until mixed thoroughly. Evenly spoon spinach mixture onto fillets. Top with sprinkles of grated lemon rind and parmesan cheese. Place baking dish into oven and bake fish 15 - 20 minutes. Fish is done when flesh is opaque in center and fish flakes easily when tested. Place slit into side of each lemon slice and garnish with twisted slice.

Muffuletta

Serves 2 - 4

1 round of sourdough bread, unsliced
⅓ lb. hard salami
⅓ lb. ham or proscuitto, thinly sliced
⅓ lb. provolone cheese, thinly sliced

Olive Salad
¾ cup green olives
¾ cup black olives
3 cloves garlic, minced
1 anchovy fillet, mashed
1 Tbsp. capers
⅓ cup fresh parsley, chopped
1 tsp. oregano
¼ tsp. fresh ground pepper
½ cup olive oil

Relish salad: To make relish, chop green and black olives very fine or to desired consistency. Mash anchovy fillet and mix in with olives. (1 tsp. anchovy paste may be substituted) Add minced garlic, capers, parsley, oregano, pepper and olive oil to olive mixture. Mix relish thoroughly and cover or seal container. Refrigerate until ready to use (can hold refrigerated for several days).

Assembly instructions: Sandwich should be assembled one day before serving. Slice bread loaf in half, horizontally; scoop out 1 inch of soft bread middle from the top and bottom of loaf. Brush inside bottom of loaf with oil from salad mixture. Layer proscuitto, salami and provolone, until ingredients heap above bottom half at least 1 inch. Generously spoon olive salad over the layered meats and cheese and top with remaining half of loaf. Press down on sandwich, put in plastic bag and tie shut. Refrigerate with weight or heavy platter on top of loaf. This helps flavors from the olive salad to permeate the entire sandwich. Refrigerating overnight is recommended. Remove sandwich 20 minutes before serving. Cut loaf into wedges before serving.

Herbed Crab Sandwich

Serves 8

2 lbs. lump crabmeat, cooked and chopped
¼ cup mayonnaise
1 Tbsp. fresh tarragon, finely chopped
1 Tbsp. fresh parsley, finely chopped
¼ cup scallions, sliced
¼ tsp. cayenne
3 dashes hot pepper sauce
8 oz. cream cheese, softened
3 eggs, beaten
2 Tbsp. Creole mustard
16 slices fresh French bread
4 large tomatoes, sliced
⅓ cup fresh shredded Parmesan cheese

In medium bowl mix together crabmeat, mayonnaise, tarragon, parsley, scallions, cayenne and hot pepper sauce. In a separate bowl beat together cream cheese, eggs and mustard. Turn on broiler. Assemble by spreading crab mixture evenly on French bread slices. Spread layer of cream cheese over crab mixture and place on baking sheet. Once all sandwiches are assembled, place baking sheet under broiler, about 6 inches from heat source, for 3 - 4 minutes. Remove from oven and carefully place tomato slices on each sandwich and lightly sprinkle with fresh parmesan. Return to broiler for another 2 minutes. Serve open faced accompanied with fresh fruit.

Fried Shrimp & Oyster Po Boy

Serves 4 - 6

2   lbs. fresh shrimp, peeled and deveined OR 1 qt. fresh oysters, drained
2   eggs
½   cup water
3   cups yellow corn flour (not corn meal)
1   Tbsp. salt
1   tsp. ground pepper
½   tsp. cayenne pepper
2   cups iceberg lettuce, shredded
•   mayonnaise
•   vegetable oil for frying
•   cocktail sauce, optional
4-6 loaves, 12" long, French bread

Wash the shrimp and place on several layers of paper towels to drain. Drain oysters in a colander. Preheat oil to 375° F. Beat eggs and water together in bowl to make an egg wash. In a separate bowl, combine corn flour, salt and peppers. First, dip shrimp or oysters in egg wash. Next, roll oysters or shrimp 6 - 8 at a time, in mixture, coating evenly. Fry oysters for about 2 minutes and shrimp about 4 minutes or until both are golden brown. Remove from oil and place on a large platter and keep warm in a 200° F oven. Allow oil to return to 375° F after frying each batch.

Warm loaves in oven, split in half length-wise and remove a little of interior from top and bottom. Spread bottom with mayonnaise and top with shredded lettuce. Fill with oysters or shrimp. If desired coat top half of loaf with cocktail sauce and place on sandwich.

Roast Beef Po Boy

Serves 4

4   lb. shoulder roast
4   cups beef stock
2   cups iceberg lettuce, shredded
4   loaves, 12 inch long, French bread
•   mayonnaise
2   tomatoes, thinly sliced

Salt and pepper roast and place on roasting rack. Slowly bake in 250° F oven for 4 - 5 hours until tender. Let roast rest on roasting rack for 30 minutes. While the roast is resting, bring beef broth to a boil. Remove roast to a carving board reserving dripping in pan. Add beef stock to dripping and scrape bottom of pan. Pour broth into a small saucepan and thicken flour and water roux. Simmer until gravy is thick. Season with fresh ground pepper and salt to taste. Slice the roast very thinly. Briefly warm the bread in a hot oven. Split loaves in half length-wise and spread generously with mayonnaise on the bottom piece. Spread about ½ cup lettuce over mayonnaise, then 6 slices of beef on lettuce. Cover with at least ½ cup of beef gravy and top with 3 to 4 slices of tomato. Cover with top half of loaf and serve.

Spicy Sweet Potato Chips

Serves 3 - 4

2   large sweet potatoes
•   vegetable or peanut oil for frying
2   Tbsp. coarse salt
2   tsp, Cajun seasoning
½   tsp. cayenne
½   tsp. paprika
¼   tsp. cumin

Combine all spices and adjust to individual palate. Pour into shaker for use later. Refrigerate potatoes for at least 1 hour. Peel potatoes and slice transparently thin. In large saucepan, pour oil to 2" depth; heat to 360° F or use a deep fat fryer with basket. Fry potatoes in small batches to a golden crisp (about 1 - 2 minutes). Remove as they brown and drain on absorbent paper. Sprinkle with seasoning mix while still hot.

Eggs Benedict

Serves 4

- 4 English muffins, split
- 2 Tbsp. butter, softened
- 8 slices of Canadian bacon
- • hollandaise sauce ingredients

Hollandaise Sauce:

- 6 large egg yolks
- ¼ cup cold water
- 1 cup salted butter, melted and kept warm
- 2 Tbsp. fresh lemon juice
- ¼ tsp. cayenne

Beat the eggs and water in a heavy 3 qt. saucepan with wire whisk. Place pan over very low heat and continue beating for 3 - 4 minutes. Yolks should become thick and pale. Pour in about 2 tablespoons of warm butter, beating constantly. Remove the pan from the heat and continue beating, adding the butter in small amounts. When you have added the last of the warm butter, return saucepan to low heat. Add the lemon juice and cayenne and beat until thoroughly incorporated. Remove from heat and keep in warm place until ready to serve. Sauce should have a glossy appearance and form very small peaks when removing whisk.

Assembly: Place buttered muffin halves on baking sheet and broil until lightly browned. Place a Canadian bacon slice on each muffin half and return to broiler just long enough to warm Canadian bacon. Place 2 muffin halves on each plate and top each with poached egg and top with hollandaise sauce. Serve immediately.

Eggs Hussarde

Serves 6

- 6 slices toasted bread, crusts removed OR toasted English muffin halves
- 6 slices baked ham, grilled
- 1½ cups Marchand de Vin sauce (pg. 61)
- 6 eggs, poached
- 1½ cup hollandaise sauce (recipe above)
- 3 tomatoes, cored, halved, seasoned and broiled

Assemble in the following order. Toast or muffin topped with grilled ham, Marchand de Vin sauce, poached egg and hollandaise sauce. Serve on warm plates accompanied by broiled tomato seasoned with salt, pepper and a light sprinkle of parmesan cheese if desired.

Eggs Sardou

Serves 6

- 3 cups creamed spinach
- 6 large artichoke bottoms (or 12 small)
- 12 eggs poached
- 3 cups hollandaise sauce (recipe above)

Put ½ cup warm creamed spinach on each plate. Place 1 or 2 warm artichoke bottoms on the bed of spinach then set 2 poached eggs on the artichoke bottoms. Cover each portion with ½ cup hollandaise sauce.

NOTES : To poach eggs, break the number of eggs you want to poach carefully in individual saucers. In a skillet or sauté pan, bring about 2 inches of water with 1 teaspoon vinegar to a slow boil. Reduce the heat just enough to keep a low boil going. Slide each egg into the water from the saucer by lowering the saucer almost to the surface of the water and tipping it. Cook each egg for about 2 to 2½ minutes in the boiling water, spooning some of the water over the surface of the eggs during cooking. When the egg is cooked, lift it out with a mesh or slotted spoon. Hold the egg over the pan for a few seconds to let the water drain off.

Pain Perdu (Lost Bread)

Serves 2

1	cup milk
2	large eggs, well beaten
¼	cup sugar
¼	tsp. vanilla extract
4	1½" slices stale French bread
2	Tbsp. salted butter
2	Tbsp. vegetable oil
½	tsp. cinnamon

In a large bowl combine the milk, beaten eggs, granulated sugar and vanilla and mix thoroughly. Soak the slices of stale French bread in the milk and egg mixture for a few minutes. Meanwhile, melt the butter in a heavy skillet and add the vegetable oil. When the butter and oil mixture are quite hot, fry the soaked bread slices one or two at a time on each side, until golden brown. Sprinkle with cinnamon sugar mixture just before serving. Serve with Louisiana cane syrup or pancake syrup if desired. Sprinkle with mixture of powdered sugar and cinnamon.

Marchan de Vin Sauce

Serves 6

½	cup salted butter
3	Tbsp. flour
¼	cup lean baked ham, finely minced
½	cup green scallion tops, finely minced
3	Tbsp. onion, finely minced
¼	cup garlic, finely minced
1	tsp. salt
¼	tsp. black pepper, freshly ground
⅛	tsp. cayenne
1	cup rich beef stock from soup bones
•	marrow from soup bones
½	cup dry red wine

In a large heavy saucepan melt the butter over low heat. Gradually add the flour stirring constantly, and cook over low heat until a light brown roux begins to form. Quickly add the ham, shallot tops, onion and garlic. Cook, still stirring, for about 5 minutes more. Add the salt, pepper, cayenne and blend thoroughly. Keep the mixture simmering and very gradually add the beef stock, bone marrow and red wine, stirring constantly to keep the sauce as smooth as possible. (It should have a slightly rough texture with the minced ham.) When the sauce is thoroughly blended, cook over very low heat for about 30 minutes, stirring from time to time to prevent scorching. Makes 2 cups.

Beignets (French Doughnuts)

Serves 12 - 14

1½	cups warm water
1	package active dry yeast
½	cup sugar
1	tsp. salt
2	large eggs
1	cup of canned evaporated milk
7	cups flour
¼	cup vegetable shortening
•	oil for deep frying
•	powdered sugar

In a large bowl dissolve yeast in warm water. Add the sugar, salt, eggs and evaporated milk. Gradually stir in 4 cups of flour and beat with a wooden spoon until smooth and thoroughly blended. Beat in the shortening, then add the remaining flour, about ⅓ cup at a time, beating it in with a spoon until it becomes too stiff to stir, then working in the rest with your fingers. Cover bowl and refrigerate overnight. Roll the dough out on a floured surface to a thickness of ⅛-inch, then cut it into rectangles 2½" x 3½" with a sharp knife. Preheat oil in a deep fryer to 360° F. Fry the beignets (about 3 - 4 minutes per batch). Turn them over in the oil once or twice to get them evenly brown. Drain each batch on absorbent paper. Sprinkle beignets heavily with powdered sugar and serve hot. Yields 4 - 5 dozen.

New Orleans Pound Cake

Serves 8 - 12

2½ cups salted butter, softened
4 cups sugar
5 cups all-purpose flour
1 tsp. baking powder
1 tsp. salt
½ cup milk
10 large eggs, room temperature
2 tsp. vanilla extract

Preheat oven to 300° F. Cream butter and sugar together in a large mixing bowl. Sift together the flour, baking powder and salt. Add sifted flour and mix into butter and sugar with wooden spoon. Gradually add the milk while continuing to slowly mix together with wooden spoon. Add eggs one or two at a time and thoroughly mix into batter. Add vanilla and thoroughly mix to evenly distribute. Butter and flour the inside of a 10" tube pan. Evenly distribute pound cake batter into tube pan and lightly tap pan on counter to remove any air bubbles. Bake for 1 hour and 20 minutes or until top is golden brown and cake tester comes out dry. After baking, cool to room temperature before turning out of pan.

Bourbon Berries

Serves 6

2 quarts ripe strawberries w/stems
½ cup bourbon
½ cup powdered sugar
1 cup heavy cream, whipped

Gently wash the strawberries and leave the stems attached. Drain. Place the berries, bourbon and powdered sugar in separate bowls. Dip the strawberries in bourbon and then in sugar. Serve accompanied by whipped cream.

Southern Peach Cobbler

Dough
2 cups all-purpose flour
1 Tbsp. sugar
½ tsp. salt
1 cup unsalted butter, chilled and thinly sliced
3 Tbsp. ice cold water

Peach Filling
12 large ripe peaches
   OR 2 lb. frozen peach slices
1 fresh lemon, juiced
¾ cup sugar
2 tsp. cinnamon
1 tsp. nutmeg
½ cup butter
3 Tbsp. flour

In a large mixing bowl sift together the dry ingredients and cut in butter until mixture resembles coarse meal. Slowly mix in just enough water to enable the dough to hold together. Shape dough into a ball, wrap, and refrigerate while preparing the peach filling. Preheat oven to 425° F. After preparing filling, roll out half of dough to fit baking dish. Pour filling over dough and roll out remaining dough to cover filling. Place dough over filling and trim off excess dough. Brush top dough with milk being careful to avoid the edges as it is likely to burn. Place a couple of slits in the top crush to allow steam to escape. Generously sprinkle with sugar before placing in preheated oven. Bake for 45 minutes or until crust is a deep golden brown. Best when served warm.

Filling: To prepare filling, peel and slice fresh peaches and toss in lemon juice. If using frozen peaches, defrost before beginning, until peaches are still frosty. Mix together sugar, cinnamon, nutmeg and flour. Sprinkle over peaches and toss until well coated. Place peaches in dough lined oven-proof skillet or baking dish.

Bread Pudding with Brandy Sauce

Serves 8 -10

1	loaf stale French bread, cubed
2½	cups whole milk
1	cup unsalted butter, softened
1¾	cups sugar
1	can evaporated milk
2	Tbsp. ground nutmeg
2	Tbsp. vanilla extract
1	cup raisins (optional)

Brandy Sauce

3	large eggs
¼	cup sugar
½	tsp. vanilla extract
¼	cup salted butter, melted
¼	cup brandy
•	dash cinnamon
½	cup whole milk

Preheat oven to 350° F. Place bread cubes in bowl and pour milk over the cubes and allow cubes to absorb the milk. Beat butter and sugar in a large bowl until light and fluffy. Beat in the evaporated milk, nutmeg and vanilla. Gently stir in the bread cubes and raisins. Place mixture into a 3 qt. casserole dish and bake for 1 hour. Stir pudding slightly and continue baking until liquid is absorbed. Best when served warm with brandy sauce (recipe below).

Brandy Sauce: Beat eggs in heavy 2 qt. saucepan. Add vanilla, sugar and butter. Heat slowly until mixture begins to thicken, stirring constantly. Remove from heat and stir in brandy, cinnamon and milk. Pour sauce into electric blender and blend on high speed for 1 - 2 minutes or until the sauce has the consistency of heavy cream.

Mardi Gras King Cake

Serves 8 - 10

1	cup milk, scalded
¼	cup cool water
1	pkg. active dry yeast
4½	cups all-purpose flour
½	lb. butter
¾	cup sugar
1	tsp. nutmeg, ground
1	tsp. lemon rind, grated
½	tsp. salt
4	large eggs at room temperature
1	small doll or prize
1	large egg
1	Tbsp. water
1	cup light corn syrup
•	colored sugars

Add ¼ cup cool water to scalded milk to make mixture lukewarm. Dissolve yeast into milk and set to side. In a large bowl, cream together butter, sugar, nutmeg, lemon rind, salt and eggs. Add milk and yeast to creamed mixture and stir until incorporated. Gradually add about 3 cups flour or until a soft dough is formed. Knead gently and place dough ball into a greased bowl. Cover and let rise in warm place until doubled in size, about 2½ hours. Knead in 1 more cup of flour for 10 minutes, adding additional flour if needed. Roll dough into a long log about 4" in diameter. Brush ends of log with water. Place dough on a greased baking sheet in the shape of an oval, connecting the ends. Insert doll or prize somewhere in the dough ring until it is undetectable. Cover again with clean damp cloth and allow to rise until doubled (about 1 hour). Preheat oven to 350° F. Mix egg with tablespoon of water to make egg wash. Brush egg wash over raised cake circle. With a sharp knife, cut 4 or 5 small slits about ½-inch deep, at a diagonal into the top of the cake. Gently place cake into oven and bake for about 40 minutes or until cake is golden brown. Remove from oven and decorate while still hot by brushing lightly with corn syrup. Immediately decorate with stripes of colored sugar and candies if desired. Slide cake onto wire rack to cool. Cut servings into 2 - 3" pieces.

Note: To make colored sugar, mix ½ cup granulated sugar with a few drops of food coloring in a resealable plastic bag. Seal bag and shake until desired tint is achieved.

ORDER FORM

If you would like to order additional copies of this book or
sample some of our other fine products, please fill out the form below and mail to:

YOUR POINT OF PURCHASE RETAILER
OR
R.A.L. ENTERPRISES
5749 Jefferson Highway, Harahan, LA 70123

TITLE	COST		QUANTITY	TOTAL
New Orleans Cuisine	**64 pgs.**	**$12.95**	_____	_____
Cajun Country Cookin'	64 pgs.	$8.95	_____	_____
Plantation Country Guide	64 pgs.	$8.95	_____	_____
New Orleans on the Mississippi River	32 pgs.	$5.95	_____	_____
Best of New Orleans Cooking	64 pgs.	$8.95	_____	_____
Favorite Recipes from New Orleans	64 pgs.	$8.95	_____	_____
Cookin' in High Cotton	64 pgs.	$8.95	_____	_____
Cookin' New Orleans Style	64 pgs.	$8.95	_____	_____
Cookin' on the Mississippi (Hard Cover)	64 pgs.	$9.95	_____	_____
Cookin' on the Mississippi (Soft Cover)	64 pgs.	$8.95	_____	_____
Historic Houses of the Deep South	64 pgs.	$12.95	_____	_____
Mississippi River Book	128 pgs.	$10.95	_____	_____
Favorite Drinks of New Orleans	32 pgs.	$5.95	_____	_____
New Orleans	64 pgs.	$8.95	_____	_____
Jazz – New Orleans Style	64 pgs.	$8.95	_____	_____
New Orleans – French Quarter	32 pgs.	$5.95	_____	_____
Laminated New Orleans Placemats	Set of 4	$9.95	_____	_____
Laminated Louisiana Plantation Placemats	Set of 4	$9.95	_____	_____
Laminated Mississippi Plantation Placemats	Set of 4	$9.95	_____	_____
Stationery Sets: 16 Notes, 16 Sheets & Envelopes			_____	_____
Mississippi Plantations	64 pieces	$9.95	_____	_____
Louisiana Plantations	64 pieces	$9.95	_____	_____
New Orleans Jazz	64 pieces	$9.95	_____	_____
French Quarter	64 pieces	$9.95	_____	_____
Recipe Box Cards	Set of 10	$5.95	Postage & Handling	$2.50
			TOTAL	_____

☐ Check Enclosed   ☐ Visa   ☐ MasterCard   ☐ American Express   ☐ Discover

Card Number _____   Expiration Date _____

Name _____

Address _____

City _____   State _____   Zip _____

Daytime Phone (___) _____

All items are satisfaction guaranteed and your purchase will be promptly refunded if returned within 30 days.
Please allow two-four weeks for delivery. No foreign orders please.